Open Thoughts

Open Thoughts

PASSAGES OF POETRY
by
Paul Ray

Sonray Press
publisher

The quotation used in the Preface of this book was written by Robert Penn Warren (1905-1989) from the Saturday Review (US Magazine), March 22, 1958.

For information, contact:
Sonray Press, 1320 Cedar Lane, Charlotte, NC 28226

Printed In the United States of America
Sonray Press First Edition

Cover and layout format by gary hixson

ISBN 978-0-578-05948-8

Dedicated to
my Mom and Dad
with love

Table of Contents

[TABLE OF CONTENTS]

Preface

In this fast paced, technologically advanced, computer and cell phone, highly capitalistic world in which we live, we are pressed on all sides and pressured at every moment. If we are not plugged into the media, constantly keeping up with the latest technological advances, the latest regulation changes or the latest corporate scandals, we believe we could miss the boat and possibly lose our shirts or skirts if we slipped out for just a moment.

We think we live on the edge of success or failure every day. We think we will sink or swim depending on how fast or how smart we work and by how much information we get and use to our advantage. It's like we are on a sinking vessel, trying desperately to climb over the tops of others just to reach a lifeboat to stay afloat. With this apparent need for speed and informational connectivity wired into our daily lives, you might ask, "What need is there anymore to read and enjoy poetry?"

May I strongly encourage you to meet this rhetorical query with a positive, even if suspicious, response. There is a great need.

Even with all the technology that goes on around us and through us at lightning speed every day, we still need, for our own emotional and spiritual well-being, to take time to let ourselves (or souls) journey and drift down the unfrequented roads of life. We still need to take time to walk in the wood, stare at the beauty of each moon phase at night with its starry backdrop, watch the ocean waves crash on the shore, look at God's splendor captured in his sunrises and sunsets, listen to a great Bach Mass and Verdi opera, view a Rembrandt and Monet painting, enjoy quiet moments meditating

while reading God's word as well as other great books of
literature and enjoy reading various types of poetic
verse. I believe that each and every one of these experi-
ences are treasures that help make life worth living.

   While I was growing up, my father repeatedly
shared one of his favorite quotes, a sage line from pro
golfer Walter Hagen, "Don't hurry or worry [Paul].
You're here for only a short time. So don't forget to stop
and smell the roses." I pray that you, dear reader, will
take time on a regular basis to stop and enjoy smelling
the roses along your path of life. My hope is that each of
the poems contained in this little book will represent
single roses given to you as a gift. Each one with its own
special beauty intended to be shared, each one opening
up with different fragrances from the images and
messages found within; and each one offering more as
one draws near, collectively opening one's mind to new
perspectives, mental aromas and fresh insights. May
God bless each of you on your journey.

   Paul Ray

"*The poem... is a little myth of man's capacity
of making life meaningful. And in the end, the poem
is not a thing we see - it is, rather, a light by which
we may see - and what we see is life.*"
   ROBERT PENN WARREN
   [1905-1989]
   Saturday Review, 22 March 1958

Open Thoughts

Leaving A Drinking Well

When we shed our earthly shell,
And we leave this earth behind;
Have we left a drinking well
Of the living water kind?

Have we lived while digging deep,
Sacrificing time and gold;
Have we made the faithful leap
Into God's warm loving hold?

Have we dipped to meet each need -
As we hear His loving call;
Scooping gifts of word and deed,
Pouring out God's love to all?

Are the talents that we share,
A refreshment to a soul;
With cool drinks to quench despair,
From the Lord who makes it whole?

Have we trusted God each day,
And allowed His streams to fill
Every one that comes our way -
Just by watching, standing still?

Is the legacy we leave
From our waters deep within;
Helping others to believe
In the Christ who cleansed their sin?

For it's only by God's grace,
That our wells will overflow;
Bubbling joy in every space,
Giving hope after we go.

Faith In Flashes

Thunder makes the ceiling quiver
In a house where children shiver
From a storm that's quickly brewing
Moving in where kids are chewing
On their sheets because they're fearful
And with faces sad and tearful;
Knowing not what will come next -
This is why they both are wrecks.
Just then lightening strikes with flashing
Causing kids to jump up, dashing
From their room each goes out wailing
Scaring dog while they go sailing
Down the hall, escaping clashes
As they both hold tearful lashes;
Dive in bed in parent's room -
This they do to hide from doom.
Mom and Dad then ease their stressin'
Holding them, they teach a lesson
How to trust in all God's power
Then and there and any hour
Listening while the storm is dying
Kids learn faith and stop their crying;
Then each child goes back to bed -
Knowing nothing's there to dread.

Learning To Serve

Remember when your mother said,
"Pick up your toys, fold down your bed,
Take out the trash, go clean the shed,
Dry dishes now, put up the bread,
Wash both your hands 'fore you are fed;"
As chores you had to do?

And then when asked, you'd quickly say,
"Aw Mom, Oh gee, why can't I play;
I have a game, if that's ok,
Please let me work another day -
I'll do them soon, oh by the way -
Could I get paid by you?"

Right after that, she gets quite mad,
And puts you in your place a tad;
Which causes shame and makes you sad,
But helps you learn to be more glad
You serve a loving Mom and Dad
Who do so much and care.

And over time when youth is 'oer,
You find that tasks are not a chore;
First learned from parents, now much more
Their gifts you offer to the Lord -
Who cleansed your heart right to the core,
Where in Christ He lives there.

All Because Of Just An Ant

Once upon a time an ant
Bit a giant elephant
On the lid of her right eye
Causing it to form a sty.
Now enraged by poorer vision
And the pain forced her decision
To find water as her mission
Which she did the next instant -
All because of just an ant.

While in river washing lid
Alligators round her hid
Looking for the perfect chance
To eat legs of elephant's.
But when gators started splashing
Elephant stomped on them, smashing
Heads on rocks then they fled, dashing
From her raging and her rant -
All because of just an ant.

Running from the river bank
Feet in mud all quickly sank
With her trunk she grabbed a branch
Which triggered an avalanche.
Tree fell down as boulders followed
In the Nile as mountain hollowed
All the gators quickly swallowed
Rock and mud mixed up with plant -
All because of just an ant.

As the waters quickly rose
Elephant could free her toes
Getting loose with chance to roam
She climbed out and headed home.
But from rocks and all the rubble
Waves went out and caused more trouble
Overflowed the dam near Jabal
Flooding fields of each peasant -
All because of just an ant.

Plants were puny on each row
Missing rain since long ago
Now the flood's a welcome sight
Bringing hope from all the blight.
Crops grew huge in all their glory
Bringing greater inventory
That's the beauty of this story -
This for Jabal, Heaven sent -
All because God used an ant.

I Thank You For Loving Today

Counseling words that you give for free
When burdened by toils and strife;
Comforting thoughts that you share with me
To brighten my view of life.

Centering only on what matters most,
And only on what gives God praise -
Cherishing moments to serve and to host;
You bless me in so many ways.

Sharpening men is the thing you do
When sharing the words of God;
Showering notes that encourage too,
With love and a gentle prod.

Sprinkling joy on each person you meet
While giving your gifts all away -
Strengthening others by washing their feet;
I thank you for loving today.

Give It To God And Trust Jesus

When stress from the pressures of life make you frown -
When friends that you've known in the past let you down;
When you've looked for work and there's none to be found -
Then give it to God and trust Jesus.

When debt and foreclosure come pounding your door -
When paying each bill is a challenging chore;
When you give it all but they ask you for more -
Then give it to God and trust Jesus.

For only in Jesus will your troubles cease -
And only in Jesus will your joy increase;
And only in Jesus will you know true peace -
So give it to God and trust Jesus.

When parenting problems begin to bring doubt -
When teens and their actions start making you shout;
When you try to love but they turn and walk out -
Then give it to God and trust Jesus.

When you have an illness that constantly strains -
When none of your doctors can help stop the pains;
When only your faith that God loves you remains -
Then give it to God and trust Jesus.

For only in Jesus will your troubles cease -
And only in Jesus will your joy increase;
And only in Jesus will you know true peace -
So give it to God and trust Jesus.

Blessings Through Cupcakes

With stirring bowl and cake mix,
Use water, eggs and oil;
Stir them together lightly
So batter will not spoil.
When mix is smooth and runny,
And blades spin 'round with ease;
Pour all the mix in separate cups,
And bake at high degrees.

While waiting on your cupcakes
Help someone feel thought of;
Make them a cup of hot tea
Or send a note of love.
Give joyfully in service
As kindness always mends,
And bless the lives of others -
Which is what God intends.

When done pull cakes from oven,
And cool them on a pan;
Get icing spread all ready,
And sprinkles in a can.
Tap all the cakes to test them -
Let coolness be their state;
Then ice the tops and sprinkle them,
And put them on a plate.

Next line them up together
And set them out with care;
While signaling to the family
For everyone to share.
Then watch the magic happen
From good things that you bake;
While little mouths and bigger ones
Eat every little cake.

Matchbooks

Matchbooks, matchbooks,
Store them in a jar;
Place them high on kitchen shelves
Right where the cookies are.
Bring them down for show and tell
And use them for a light;
But never leave them laying 'round
And keep them out of sight.

Matchbooks, matchbooks,
Holding wicks that burn;
Used for good, they give us warmth
And light at every turn.
But if they fall in the wrong hands
A house or wood destroy;
For they could be a dangerous thing
If treated like a toy.

Matchbooks, matchbooks,
Store them dry and clean;
If you save the vintage ones
They're treasures, if pristine.
Display them in a shadow box
With packs from long ago;
Enjoy their parts in history
With different adds they show.

Matchbooks, matchbooks,
Their blaze will never last;
Like joys and blessings in our lives -
They come and go so fast.
But strike a match within your heart
And spread eternal fire;
By sharing love to everyone
Which is the Lord's desire.

Healing The Heart

When you know you've hurt another
Do not let time pass you by;
Go right to that injured brother -
Share your sin with tearful eye.

If your sister is in sorrow
Comfort her with open arms;
Give her love, don't wait tomorrow
This is one of heaven's charms.

Time's too short to waste on grudges
Who knows when your life is through;
Let God's love erase the smudges
Of all the sins and hurts in you.

God's the heart and soul physician
You can only ease the pain;
If you love and have the mission
Live for Christ and never wane.

Climbing A Tree

The grasp of flaky bark holds strong
My hands while pulling to ascend;
Each step avoids the brittle song
Of cracking that would bring my end.

I hit a branch and strike a knee,
Which causes it to bleed and bruise;
Still I keep climbing up the tree,
While getting panoramic views.

Then perched up high I look around
To see what eagles would behold;
The place where wind's the only sound,
And lakes below all gleam in gold.

The clouds hold light where rays outpour
While getting close to Heaven's space;
I stretch my hands as if to soar,
And brush against my Father's face.

The wind blows through my hands and hair
As I enjoy this peaceful rest;
But soon descent will be the bear
That I must tame with careful zest.

Though way up in a tree with views
Of gleaming lakes and clouds with rays;
Far greater sights 'wait those who choose
To serve the Lord with faithful praise.

Eight Times The Earth Went 'Round The Sun

Eight times the earth went 'round the sun -
Our world had only just begun
To know a parent's joy;
To have and hold and kiss a face,
And feel a child's sweet warm embrace
While under God's employ.

The time we had was brief but bright
With toys and games and walks at night,
And pitches on the lawn;
What zest for life he showed so well,
Who ran in fields like a gazelle
Or like the nimblest fawn.

But then one day a storm arose,
And struck our child from head to toes
From fever and a chill;
In haste the doctors tested him,
Which proved his chance to live was slim
With no known cure or pill.

O precious child who lay in bed,
With wrinkled brow and fevered head,
A rose among wild flowers;
We came to him and held his hand,
And kissed his face where tears did land
On cheeks for many hours.

I still recall the words my son
Spoke last as I had just begun
To brighten up his room;
"Do not be sad. I'm here with God
With clothes so white and joy abroad,
Forever from this gloom."

Right then his life was taken there,
Assuring us not to despair
Of where his soul was sent;
And now we wait upon the Lord -
While trusting Him in deed and word,
As our lives now are spent.

Different Choices

Although time is constant still,
As each grain falls one by one;
God has given us free will -
Spending dash for self or Son.

Pressed when tempted we give in,
Making choices in the heat;
Failing to seek counsel then -
Stumbling, rising, then repeat.

This, the road that most men take,
Running towards a greater strife;
Blinded by the gold they make -
And in rags then after life.

But a choice, however small,
With God's blessing will unfold;
Treasures poured from Heaven's hall -
Which guide souls to streets of gold.

Sweet Peace

When curves of life are treacherous and tempt you to give in -
Remind yourself who's gone that road before;
When trials become so challenging there's no way to begin -
Remember Christ already won the war.

The struggles here on earth it seems go on and never cease -
There's war and famine there at every turn;
Christ is the one who brings a cure and offers lasting peace
When you give all your heart to him and learn.

No sooner do you trust someone than they will let you down,
And give you an excuse for their offense;
If only you would learn to trust in Christ, the heavenly crown -
The joy you get would always be intense.

So keep your eyes on Jesus Christ and never look away -
He'll keep you on the road to heaven's shore;
Give Christ the troubles in your life that's made you go astray -
Then you will have sweet peace forevermore.

Comics Under Covers

I would read my books for hours
With the sheets over my head;
Holding flashlight on the pages
Of my comic books in bed.

Imitating sounds of gunshot
As Dick Tracy's pistol fired;
I would shout words of excitement
Every time a crook retired.

Then my parents gave a warning
From the family room below;
"Someone better be asleep now
Since it's time for Johnny's show!"

I would quickly turn down volume
Knowing now my parents knew
I was up way past my bedtime,
Which I often tried to do.

After that I glanced at Richie,
Scrooge McDuck, Bugs and Sad Sack;
All tucked underneath my covers
With Batman, piled in a stack.

While I read about the Joker
Throwing vial at Robin's feet;
Gas poured out to start him laughing -
This caused me to then repeat.

As I laughed, the sound of footsteps
Shuffled up the stairs and hall;
Hearing this, I turned my lamp off
As I froze curled in a ball.

Dad came in and turned the light on
And said, "Not another peep!
I want all your books put up now
And want you to go to sleep!"

At that, books were put in bookcase
Then Dad turned off bedroom light;
Closing door once I was tucked in
He then wished one last good night.

But when Dad had walked back downstairs
Right after he shut the door;
With my Spiderman night vision
In the dark, read Mighty Thor.

Treasure In The Darkness

Darkness comes while I repose in stillness -
Cold winds chill and ice my window pane;
Ambers glowing red to warm the illness,
While I hear the sound of freezing rain.

Now alone my thoughts begin to hover
Of the buds and daffodils of spring;
Gentle winds that kiss the fields and clover -
Beauty fills my thoughts while listening.

Though the world is bleak from winter's duty,
I am cloaked in quilts of green and red;
Made by mother's loving hands with beauty,
And each signed by her in silken thread.

In the hearth the smoke drifts up like phantoms -
Forming images to visualize;
As it curls and moves it looks like Bantams,
With great beaks and wings that slowly rise.

Then the pain transcends my strength to languish,
As I cough from my pneumonia spells;
Hand to mouth I brace and wretch in anguish
From the rasping plight a lung foretells.

But the silence comes again while drinking
Some hot Russian tea with lemon peel;
Then I lay my head back while I'm thinking
How I'm blessed despite the way I feel.

Looking at the cards lined on my dresser -
From my family who love me so;
I can see that I have far more treasure
Than the kings of men will ever know.

Cat Paws

Cat paws stretched out on the floor
Showing pads that I adore
Soft as satin do they feel
As I rub their lower heel.
Some paws come with fluffy hair
Which shed on the couch and chair
Other paws have tiny feet
With dark pads under their seat.
They are swift to swat a ball
Making noises in the hall
Chasing after moths and bees
As they play piano keys.
Paws spread wide up in the sky
Swatting flies as they pass by
Oh what fun and constant joy
Watching them pounce on a toy.

Cat paws on a bowl of fish
Tapping glass as tetras swish
Fun to watch as laughter pours
Spying paws slide under doors.
Velvet pads touch stairs at night
Walking up and down each flight
Other paws are licked with care
As they're used to groom their hair -
Cleaning ears and back of head
Just as kitty goes to bed.
Paws go digging in a rug
Claws come out and give a tug
And another thing they do
While you sit, they knead on you.
But just like a rose's touch -
Beware the thorns; they hurt so much.

Sharing God's Word

I used to think that I could not
Share Jesus with you friend -
Because I knew I'd risk a lot
And watch our friendship end.

I thought by saying that I care
Was all I had to say
To make you open up and share
And help you find your way.

As time passed by I'd realize
That listening's not enough -
Because I heard the same old cries
To rid the same old stuff.

I prayed for you one stormy night
That you would come around;
But heard God say, "Go be a light
And share what you have found."

I jumped up and put on my shoes -
The act was out of love;
I had to tell you of the news
Of Christ the Lord above.

I ran in rain and took a spill -
My wet clothes all drenched through;
But I was on a mission still
To share God's love with you.

I rang your bell with Word in tow -
You saved me from the showers;
And as we sat with hot cocoa,
We read God's word for hours.

You read the scriptures and obeyed
The gospel finally;
And now you're His which Christ has paid
With blood to set you free.

Give thanks to God and Christ alone
For your salvation story;
And praise His name and praise His throne
Through Christ who brings Him glory.

Your life has changed since now you know
How to be born again;
Now take the torch; be bold and go
And take God's word to men!

Matilda The Wonder Dog

Dreary day spent under covers
With a fever in my bed;
Glancing out my bedroom window,
Pain from laughter hurt my head.
There I saw my neighbor's hound dog
Rolling down the street on skates;
Being pushed and pulled by children,
Which of course a canine hates.
But Matilda was quite gracious
Letting kiddies roll her 'round;
Even with a red cape fastened,
She just rolled without a sound.
Up and down the street she glided
As her cape flapped in the breeze;
I was rolling now from laughter,
Falling down upon my knees.
Then Matilda started howling,
Which came not as a surprise;
She was trying to say, "I've had it."
You could see it in her eyes.
All at once she lost her balance,
And she stumbled in a ditch;
Skates flew off with cape entangled,
As a boy went to unhitch.
Soon Matilda ran from torment
And the wheels tied to her feet;
She dove quickly in her dog house,
Which to her was a retreat.
After that I felt much better
From the laughter and the ache;
For the Wonder Dog Matilda
Caused my temperature to break.

When 'Ere I Gaze Into Her Eyes

When 'ere I gaze into her eyes
I seem to stand there paralyzed
By two bright jewels that mesmerize
Me there while in a crowd.

And as she holds me in her trance
My heart inside begins to dance
For when a smile forms by her glance
Then I drift on a cloud.

These precious eyes are like a child
Both full of life and slightly wild
But with great love that has beguiled
My heart to feel this way.

Oh lovely eyes - they're so divine
Because they love and make me shine
And say she'll be my valentine
Forever and a day.

Because Of Your Beauty

A league of God's angels descended,
Rejoicing and singing in bands;
The moment they glanced at your beauty,
And saw what God gave with his hands.

It was not your lovely appearance
That made all the seraphs rejoice,
But it was your inward most beauty,
And love that you gave as your choice.

Your chest held a heart full of treasure
That poured out with beautiful gems;
You blessed everyone that you talked to
Embracing each stranger like friends.

Your tears were like shimmering diamonds
When shared with those who were in pain;
You dined with the sinners and outcast
And loved them again and again.

Your eyes were like two precious sapphires
That glistened while searching for needs;
You gave up your gold to the hurting
While sharing miraculous deeds.

Your mouth poured out pearls of great wisdom
That brought both great peace and a sword;
You gave out more rubies and emeralds
While speaking the truth from God's Word.

You knew that you came from the Father
To live and to die for our sin;
You now sit with God up in heaven
And wait for us there now. Amen.

A Little Bit About Angels

An angel glows with light so bright it's hard for us to see
An angel comes to show the way and comforts you and me
An angel blows his trumpet loud when there's some news to tell
An angel warns the wrath of God that bring the fires of hell
An angel is a messenger that tells God's holy plan
An angel gives encouragement to those who need a hand
An angel could be someone new we run up to and greet
An angel could be the next one we pass by on the street
An angel came at different times found in the word of God
An angel came in many forms, both beautiful and odd
An angel spoke to Abraham to stop his sacrifice
An angel gave Manoah's wife some news and sound advice
An angel came to Moses in a bush of flaming fire
An angel forced Sennacherib to withdraw and retire
An angel came to Hagar's side when forced from Abram's wife
An angel watched a lion's den and guarded Daniel's life
An angel made a donkey scared to walk or move her head
An angel came to Gideon and burned the meat and bread
An angel came to shepherds while they watched their sheep one night
An angel warned of Herod so a family could take flight
An angel moved a stone away and gave some guards a scare
An angel told some women Christ arose and wasn't there.

Most angels serve our God above in glory and in song
And help the people here on earth and watch them all day long
But once there was an angel who fought God in Heaven and lost
Who was thrown out with his demons and cast down at a cost
His name is Satan in this world who tries to win our soul
But Christ has conquered him for us, who saves and makes us whole.

The Gitchy Gitchy Goo

In the jungles of the Long Laffmenny -
By the river of the Flimflampoo;
Near a mountain called the Wooyaskinny,
Are the people called the Gitchy Gitchy Goo.

They are happy folk with cheeks like cherries -
They have rings of gold that hang under their nose;
They eat fancy food that's mixed with berries,
And their feet always have sand between their toes.

When the women folk cook Goo fried liver,
Then the men will hunt an antelope or boar;
And the children go bring sand in from the river,
For a festival that night they have in store.

Later on they get the tables ready
As the men prepare a fire and cook the beast;
Then they eat cooked bamboo like it is spaghetti
While the children bring out goat milk for the feast.

When they all sit down there's silence then a blessing,
Then they eat up all the boar with its big snout;
After that they eat leaf salad with some dressing,
Then they all jump up to dance and sing and shout.

"Goo Roo Goo Roo Gitchy Gitchy Goo
Rumbo Gumbo Ne-Kee Le-kee Loo
Nak-ki Raki-ki Mik-ki Nau-To-Rae
Humbo Gumbo Ne-kee-Me-Lo Say!"

30

Then drums go "bum bum bum bum" as their sounding
While the sand is spread out over on the floor;
Then they dance on sand to soften all the pounding
As they stomp and sing to God again once more.

"Goo Roo Goo Roo Gitchy Gitchy Goo
Rumbo Gumbo Ne-Kee Le-kee Loo
Nak-ki Raki-ki Mik-ki Nau-To-Rae
Humbo Gumbo Ne-kee-Me-Lo Say!"

As they sing this verse and others 'round the campfire,
With the flames all shooting straight up toward the sky;
Faith is seen where missionaries did inspire
From the words they sing to God who's up on High.

"The people of the Gitchy Gitchy Goo
All thank you God for everything you do
Not one of us is worthy of your light
But help us God be pleasing in your sight!"

A Thank You Note To God

There is no way to thank you God
For all that you have done;
You always give such perfect gifts
That bless us one by one.

We thank you for your precious word
That shows the perfect way
To live for you and honor you
While serving every day.

We thank you for each worship time
To praise you when we sing;
And for our Christian family
For all the love they bring.

The money, health and things we have
Are borrowed and are yours;
Along with food that's on our shelves
And all the clothes from stores.

Our moms and dads are precious gifts
You've given from above;
With siblings, spouse and children, too
All sent from you with love.

We thank you for the happy times
And victories while we live;
Each day is a thanksgiving day
From all the joy you give.

We thank you God for trials, too -
Which help us persevere;
They're tests to build a stronger faith
And teach us not to fear.

But there in all the gifts you give
With love that never ends;
We thank you most of all for Christ
Who washed away our sins.

Door Breezes

Not many summers in the past,
As family we would go
To see the whales swim at Sea World
And watch the dolphin show.

And other times we'd go on trips
Like Knoxville or DC;
And play Putt-Putt, or ride the tram,
Or go to a movie.

But nowadays when school is out
For summertime recess,
My teenagers are always gone
On teenage trips, I guess.

For when my son comes through the door
From surfing Onslow Bay;
I ask how long he'll be at home,
To which he states, "One day."

Or when my daughter smiles at me
When asked, "How 'bout we shop?"
And then she says most sheepishly,
"I'm leaving, but thanks Pop."

My kids come in and out our doors
So fast they make a breeze;
I swear they fan and cool the house
By five or ten degrees.

I guess I didn't realize
How fast the time goes by;
My kids both want to spread their wings,
To leave the nest and fly.

So every time I sit at home
Awaiting latch to lift;
And see my child come through the door,
I praise God for His gift.

Working And Walking For Jesus

When you're busy while you're working
Is your love for people shirking?
When you're rushing,
Are you brushing
Past the hurting at their post?

Do you jump to serve another
Even if they're not your brother;
Without meaning,
To be screening
Just the ones who like you most?

Don't you know the satisfaction
Being Jesus live in action
As you're caring,
While you're sharing
Of the cross and His abuse?

Are you loving while you're walking
And share God's word while you're talking?
Or while praying,
Are you saying,
"It's not my gift," your excuse?

Just beware of Bible knowledge
That you learn at church or college;
While your stuffing,
Could cause puffing
Which could turn a friend away.

But just love the way Christ teaches
And you'll bless as God's word reaches
Hearts with healing,
As you're kneeling,
Lifting prayers to God each day.

Stop And Listen

Stop and listen every day
To hear your Father's voice;
He speaks to you in everything
But you must make the choice.
He talks to you in nature and
In all of mankind's plays;
And if you listen very close
He'll bless you all your days.
Stop and hear Him every morn
Through songs the cardinals sing;
And hear each tender aria
God gives as His blessing.
The tapping of the woodpecker
And cooing of the dove;
Are different sounds your Father makes
Given to you with love.
Stop and hear Him in a crowd
With murmurs in the air;
And hear Him through your family
With wisdom that they share.
Listen close to friend and foe
For guidance will be found
That God has whispered in your ear;
So recognize His sound.
Stop and listen to God's words
And learn to trust in them;
For if you follow His advice
You'll grow in His wisdom.
Pray that you will comprehend
To understand His will;
And always on His frequency
While quietly standing still.

The Primrose Path

The journey down the primrose path
Brings perfume and a sauna bath;
With flashy cars and diamond rings,
And night clubs, yachts and meals with kings.

There's trips abroad and fancy hair,
And mansions with a porte-cochere;
But it's the road the wise can see
Brings sudden death and poverty.

That darkened path feeds heart's desire,
And when it's blocked, folks then conspire
To feed it by some other means -
Which sometimes starts by making scenes.

They'll rant and rave and get all bent,
While arguing their entitlement;
And when they win the thing they want,
They'll wave it with a spiteful flaunt.

This is to say, "Don't mess with us!
You lose. Go home. Get on the bus."
But though it seems they've won the war,
A dismal loss is soon in store.

For though this path seems rosy red,
With comforts, wealth and trips ahead;
There comes a day they'll all lay bare,
And not a soul or God will care -

About the wealth or degrees earned -
And all the trips with language learned;
For there the primrose path is gone,
And they'll be judged for all they've done.

For if our lives are spent on self,
There will not be eternal wealth;
But only life in misery -
Cut off from God eternally.

So choose a life on Jesus' path,
And He will spare you from the wrath;
You'll always be of royalty -
Because you're in God's family.

Haloes

I drifted high to Heaven's gate,
And walked into a potentate,
Who told me that I must be blue
Since haloes 'round my head were few.
I asked him how to gain some more,
But he walked on and did ignore
My inquiry about my ring,
Which seemed to be a "novice thing."
I then walked over clouds awhile
With heavy heart and half a smile,
But angels sensed the stress in me,
And came over immediately.
They knew at once my glow was out,
With lips that formed a heavy pout.
"Dear saint, you seem so deep in thought;
We came to find out what has brought
You so much trouble to your head
Since you have nothing here to dread."
I looked up in their eyes afire,
And spoke and shared my heart's desire;
"I'd like more haloes and more rings
So I'd not stick out like your wings!"
Then all the angels spoke and said,
"Each saint here has one ring per head.
Please tell us where you heard this news
Since we would like to end this ruse."
Describing king, not long ago,
Who pointed out my lone halo,
I told them how it came to pass
He condescended with his sass.
Then all the angels flew away
While asking that I'd simply pray;

So there I bowed on clouds and knees
And thanked God for servants like these.
It wasn't long 'til angels came
Back with a king, that was the same
Who gave me grief not long ago
About my single ring halo.
He came at once to me and said
While looking at my haloed head,
"I'm sorry you misunderstood,
When I was trying to do you good.
I said your 'head glows' dim in size
Which means you need to just arise
And sing with praises to the Lord
For all his blessings and His word.
Remembering all the joy He brings;
The God of love and King of Kings.
And when you glow, your ring will too
Because you let God shine in you.
God loves you. This forever know…
Stand and sing and you will glow!"
And with these words, the king was gone
While leaving me to think alone;
In just a flash, my head had cleared
For Christ just spoke to me and steered
My focus back on Him again
Who is my Savior from my sin.
I stood at once and sang out loud
All songs with joy and feeling proud
To be in God's great family
While praising Him for loving me.
And in an instant I did know
My head beamed bright from my halo.

Itching Ears

Be careful having itching ears
That side with trends and thoughts of peers;
Because their views can be off track -
Swayed by acceptance of the pack.

When hearing words pressed to agree
Make truth your first priority;
And find out where that person found
The source that made their words profound.

For if the truth is not attained
Then you'll be glad you've learned and gained
One more hypothesis of man
That does not follow God's life plan.

Watch out when people try to make
You walk a path you should not take;
And seek out first, with much advice
About the road that seems so nice.

Remember when the serpent said,
"Eve, eat the fruit. You'll not be dead.
You'll be like God with great wisdom."
At that, Eve should have turned and run.

And since that time so long ago
Men still want ways that they can show
That they are right and they fit in -
But disregard God's cure for sin.

So train your ears and listen well
To hearts of men where words will tell
What path they're on or soon will find
If you don't help them change their mind.

Prepare yourself and know the cure
When myths and itching ears endure;
And follow just God's word each day
Despite what sage or friend may say.

For when you do, great things will start
Beginning with a Christ-like heart;
You'll listen well with loving ears -
And now and then correct with tears.

We Are Brothers

We are brothers in this place
We are brothers by God's grace
We are here to love each day
And are here to serve and pray
Called to act when there's a need
Giving hope with word and deed
Even when we're down and out
We show what true love's about
Spreading peace and hope around
We're in Christ and heaven bound.

I'm your brother in this life
I'm your brother through the strife
Fighting Satan every day
Guarding you along the way
As we serve the perfect light
I'm your keeper to what's right
If you stumble and do wrong
I'll forgive you all day long
If the darkest pit you fall
I will help to lift you tall.

You're my brother reaching high
You're my brother in the sky
Filled with love you give God praise
You're my brother and always
As I watch I know you are
Shining bright both close and far
Where you stay or God will send
You're my brother and my friend
But of all the truths thereof
God has blessed me with your love.

New Jerusalem

Glittering gates and shimmering curtain walls of white -
Bastions rising through clouds that scintillate and glow;
Spiraling finials shooting rays of beaming endless light
Through golden skies with winds that gently blow.
Within these gates and arcades which God above has cast,
Whose splendor fills each ward and every mighty hall;
His brilliance dulls the gold around Him in contrast -
Forever shining on each door and Elysium wall.
The royal saints of God are crowned in loving grace
While angels chant with praises standing wing to wing;
The Son of God comes with His love and His embrace,
And every saint is kissed by Christ the King.
Those that follow the Lord will then soon have a place
In the promised New Jerusalem rejoicing.

Laugh And Pray At Home

I love my children's laughter while I'm in the other room -
To hear them giggle while they watch TV;
It lifts my heart to know their souls are filled with mirth, not gloom,
Because their joy means everything to me.

To hear the sound of silence broken by a burst of cheer -
Along with tapping happy little feet;
Bring little aggravation in our home throughout the year,
For wife and I both view them as a treat.

I treasure children chuckling while trying to go to bed,
And after, hear a child call up to me;
"Dad, come and listen to a joke that Mom picked up and read" -
At that, I quickly join my family.

The timbre made by sonny's howl or daughter's quick outpour,
Bring instant joyful feelings in our house;
And sometimes when we pray at home I fall down on the floor
From laughing caused by tickles from my spouse.

I think that laughter in the home is vital every day
To form a stronger bond in each one's lives;
For if more time was spent at home to gather, laugh and pray,
God would restore more husbands to their wives.

God loves to hear us laughing in our home and everywhere -
It is His gift that heals right to the bone;
So laugh out loud with all your kin and join in daily prayer,
For families heal and grow in God alone.

Sweet Precious Lamb

Sweet precious lamb who died just for me -
A root that grew up in dry lands;
Your sinless life hung up on a tree,
While nailed by both feet and both hands.
Despised and rejected you held it all in -
A lamb sheared in silence and still;
Though tortured and slaughtered by great sinful men,
You knew it was your Father's will.
Oh lamb of God, you suffered the most
When God turned his face from your view;
You cried out in pain as you gave up the ghost,
While paying for sins that were due.
Wrapped in some linen and put in a grave
You lay there entombed as we've read;
Then after three days passed the world did you save
By rising again from the dead.

Has Someone Ever Told You?

Has someone ever told you how much you look like Jesus?
Has someone ever told you how much you love like Him?
Has someone ever thanked you for mending all the pieces
From hurting hearts which you've restored again?

Have people ever mentioned how bright your star is shining?
Have people ever mentioned how blessed they are with you?
Have people ever told you that your love is redefining
How a person who's a "Christian" should act, too?

You have a joy about you that all find so refreshing.
You have a joy about you that all are looking for.
You have the joy that Jesus shared to everyone expressing
That completes each life in Him forevermore.

So keep on being Jesus while being love in motion,
And keep on being Jesus while serving as you pray;
Keep loving and abiding in the Lord with great devotion,
So all will share eternity someday.

God Is There

As the wisp comes from the pool
And the sunlight crests the pine
As the jasmine springs renewal
And a zephyr's mist is fine
While in stillness sounds a dove
And the forest stirs with air
Causing leaves to dance above -
It's a gift, for God is there.

As the mountains tinge with red
And the stalks hold out each flower
As the geese fly overhead
And the clouds provide a shower
When the crane dips in a rill
And the doe grooms back its hair
While the buck is standing still -
It's a gift, for God is there.

As the sun melts in the west
And the moonlight starts to grow
When the owl swoops from its nest
And the fireflies flash and glow
When the wolf lifts out a cry
And a star falls like a flare
Streaking light across the sky -
It's a gift, for God is there.

Standing In Line For Ice Cream

There I stand in line and tarry
Hearing children often scream;
It's a day when Ben and Jerry
Give away some free ice cream.

Nudging, shuffling ever closer
To the counter for a taste;
Longing for a seat or bolster
And a wish that they'd make haste.

With blue skies above I wonder
Why I stand there doing this;
All at once my heart's asunder
When I feel my daughter's kiss.

"Thank you," were the words next stated
As she held me with a smile;
My head cleared as now I waited
Patiently from her beguile.

Children passed us while all eating
Ice cream just outside our reach;
As they did my heart was beating
Wishing for a scoop of peach.

Soon we both stepped in to order
Ice cream from the list they had;
Daughter found an unclaimed quarter
While we both ate feeling glad.

Times like these are always treasured
With my children and my wife;
These are times that can't be measured
And have value all my life.

So when you're in line and dating
With your wife or child as such;
Just recall it's worth the waiting
And will bless you both so much.

Branson Brody

Branson Brody died one day
While jostling Juliette far away
From crashing curtains in a play
That pulled down on his head.

Rafters rocked as beams broke free
That caused the drape calamity,
And doused Shakespeare's soliloquy -
With Branson cloaked and dead.

Juliette jested god of sun
To whip his steeds so they would run
In westward haste, as beams begun
To drop down on the stage.

But as her Phaethon pleads came out -
A stagehand rushed her with a shout,
And saved her skin, without a doubt -
A hero of the age.

The actors and the owners stayed
With Branson's wife for weeks and prayed,
While every funeral bill was paid
By guild and understudy.

And from then on at curtain calls,
When cheers and screams ring out from walls;
The actors shout throughout the halls -
"God bless you Branson Brody!"

Riding On Moonbeams

Sleep now in slumber and ride on moonbeams,
Soft in your cradle, the ship of your dreams;
Rising and floating away in the air,
Drifting while angels watch over you there.

Hear now their singing as you sail on by,
Fanning your sails with their wings in the sky;
Swinging you upward to drift to the stars,
Passing a planet of red that's called Mars.

Sailing through comets you travel with ease,
Circling the moon with an angel wing's breeze;
Cruising and gliding in your little bed,
There you lie gently my sweet curly head.

Rest now my baby for God's guiding you -
He is your captain and comforter too;
Bringing you safely back home from above,
Steering your ship while He wraps you with love.

A Shopping Experience

Rushing down a lane while shopping
Greta stopped her child from hopping
On a shiny Hot Wheel cycle
Which was just the thing her Michael
Wanted most on Christmas morning
That he showed her without warning
With bike pictures during her bath
In wedding frames that caused her wrath.

Now she stood in the toy section
Trying to make a gift selection
Among Barbies, Jacks and Tiggers
While her son grabbed action figures
From a shelf that caused them crashing
Down on Greta's head while smashing
Super heroes on the floor
With Batman, Hulk and Mighty Thor.

While she stood amongst the messes
She saw scouts in skirts and dresses
Coming to her rescue filing
As a group of Girl Scouts piling
All the boxes back precisely
Just the way they were so nicely
On the shelves while having fun
And as they left, she thanked each one.

Greta was inspired by seeing
Children trained to serve while being
Cheerful givers to the stressing
Any time a need was pressing
So because of her elation
Greta sent a gift donation
To the Girl Scouts since they care
And for the principles they share.

Embrace The Time Before Us

Life is short and Satan's against us,
Who has spread great pain on the earth;
It began with lies in the Garden,
And has plagued each man from his birth.

But then God sent Christ as the savior
To redeem mankind once again;
For this hope is found in His gospel -
To obey Christ and follow Him.

As disciples of Christ our Savior,
We are called to spread the good news;
Sharing love and truth to each person
Careful not to judge, pick or choose.

Let's embrace the time that's before us,
And resolve to give God our best;
For if we serve Him in our weakness
He will come and fill in the rest.

Moving out with faith turned to action,
Spreading seeds of hope everywhere;
Being light for Christ all around us -
Asking God's empowerment in prayer.

Let us live each day for the Master,
Let us keep our hearts from desire;
Let us speak the truth in each lesson,
Let us spread His love like a fire.

So when each is called home to glory,
And when each one bows at His throne;
God will fold up time in His pocket,
And will claim us each as His own.

Gentle Words With Healing Power

Healing hurts are never fun, but
It's a need, so I've begun with
Crumpled papers on the floor from
Poor attempts to write down more than
Simple words describing ways to
Aid someone who hurts and stays with
Anger in their hearts from sin so
Here it goes, let this sink in.

Bitterness becomes the mood when
Those you love are being rude, then
Walk away like they don't care and
Look back with a heartless stare which
Triggers anger in your brain and
Makes you want to go insane, but
Then you act like you ignore them,
Planning ways to tie the score.

This may seem a way to fight, but
May I give a different light that
Is a way to soften blows when
You just want to punch their nose in
Front of them and with their friends, which
Only harms and never mends the
Hurting, so consider this - Speak
Gentle words of true kindness.

Hostility is often mean when
Loved ones fight and leave the scene and
Never try to reconcile or
Talk it out and stay awhile, which
Leaves each member torn inside and
Puts up walls from hurtful pride that
Lashes out with acid tongue and
Notches anger up a rung.

When this hurt wells deep within, I
Urge you, and I say again, to
Hold your tongue and count to three and
Think of ways to gently be a
Set of ears who wants to hear, a
Broad shoulder who rests a tear, a
Head that's bowed in silent prayer, and
Gentle words that show you care.

Enjoy Each New Day

Enjoy each new day
Slow down in your stride
Breathe in some fresh air
Set some time aside
Go out for a walk
Where flowers all bloom
Blow bubbles, fly kites -
Paint or write in your room.
Play games on the lawn
Like croquet on the grass
Enjoy picnic lunch
Sip tea from a glass
Turn the radio on
To classical strings -
And listen while reading
Or snacking on wings.
Sit down by a lake
Watch fish swim around
Skip rocks at the shore
To help get unwound
Go watch a sunset
As it changes hue -
Then thank God for giving
Each moment to you.

Welcome Home Son

We're glad you're home.
And know you're tired -
Enjoy yourself this week;
Put down your bags,
Bring out the food -
It's R&R you seek.

Go take a bath,
And get unwound -
Plop down and watch TV;
Lie on your bed,
Turn on some tunes -
Enjoy your family.

Your room has changed,
The décor, too -
With office files and gear;
But even so,
You have a bed,
And home is always here.

We've missed you so,
For months on end,
And almost come undone;
But since you're home,
We celebrate,
And welcome you, dear son.

Keep Pressing On

Press on, oh child of God - you're almost home!
Do not allow life's chaos to deter your call;
No matter when the trials or grief may come -
Both great and small; It's worth it all.
Keep pressing on!

Hold high your shield of faith with armor all in place;
Though bullets of oppression may impact with lead -
Salvation takes the blow protecting crown and face -
Or you'd be dead; So look ahead.
Keep pressing on!

Wave on Christ's freedom flag through every victory,
And let His words of power attract abroad;
It is truth's belt and sword which changes you and me -
The word of God; A lightening rod.
Keep pressing on!

Lift up the hurt and fallen as you're passing by,
And show them love by having gospel feet;
Point them to Jesus on the cross and tell them why -
Through death's defeat; New life complete.
Keep pressing on!

Your Touch Is Springtime

Your touch is springtime flowers to my day -
As is your spirit fresh air to my soul;
Your faith in Jesus blesses you this way -
Adorned in Heaven, sanctified and whole.
Your words bring comfort to each hurting scar -
That smooth away the marks through loving rhyme;
The tasks you do each day, though menial are -
No more than gifts of love you share each time.
You shine for God as His celestial star
And make each ordinary task sublime.
Reverberating love is all you do -
While deep inside rejoicing in His grace;
Your faith turns every stormy sky to blue
And brings each soul to God and his embrace.

A Smile

A smile is just a little gift we all can give away,
That doesn't cost us anything while brightening someone's day;
It is a thing that comes from God that heals all weary souls,
And is contagious like a flame that fires up dying coals.
When shared, it will illuminate each room and darkened place,
By spreading all its beauty as it lights up every face;
It's lifted hearts in battle and it lessens daily trial,
So never underestimate the power that's in a smile.

Star Of Wonder

Star of wonder shining bright
In the darkness of the night
With a beam fine tuned in space
Guiding Magi to the place
Where the Jewish king did live
For to worship and to give
Gold and myrrh and frankincense
Known as Christ's first birth presents.
Star of wonder to one's sight
Just to bring the wise delight
Showing men of noble birth
The great gift to all the earth
Sent from God to save all men
Staying there in Bethlehem
Little king whose death would be
Man's one hope for liberty.
Star of wonder shining bright
Holy beacon toward true Light.

Temporal Dreams

Within a man lies temporal dreams
Of power, wealth and fame;
Which gratify a common wish
To rise above the game.

A man who seeks to be a king
Must watch his back each day;
For even those who're close to him
Could take his throne away.

A foolish and recurring plight
That man with means acquire;
They never seem to have enough
To quench their wealth desire.

And then there is the famous man
Whose made his mark, and yet -
A generation passes by
And people all forget.

Beware in following temporal dreams
For they bring grief and strife
And have no worth with no coins saved
Up in your afterlife.

But dream you'll make a mark for Christ
And not for men on earth;
Put all your stock in heavenly things -
Then God will give you worth!

Be careful then the dreams you seek
And know their consequence;
Seek only those that praise the Lord -
Divine as you commence.

Being Meek

Pleasant words bring healing faster
When the stress of conflict's high;
Gentle tones avoid disaster -
Soothing like a lullaby.

Watching, waiting, for the moment
To speak up and meet a need;
Letting words of God's atonement
Stir a heart and plant a seed.

In the scriptures Christ in silence -
Kneeling, writing, in the sand;
Stood with question countering violence,
Bowed again, but broke the band.

So be quick to stoop while hearing,
And in love be slow to speak;
This is how God wants us steering
Souls to Christ - by being meek.

A Picnic With My Wife

Driving through the countryside
With wife next to my seat;
We looked ahead for a nice spot
So we could sit and eat.
The hills had flowers everywhere;
It was a perfect day -
But shade was difficult to find
Since trees were far away.

It wasn't long my wife did spy
A tree both big and red;
With giant trunk and outstretched limbs
And leaves to shade our head.
The only problem with the tree
Was it's location there -
Within a fence that had some barbs
And sign that said "beware."

I pulled the car off to the side
And went to have a look;
The shade was cool beneath the tree
With flowers near a brook.
I saw where we could step across
The fence without a slice -
And thought the sign warned of the spurs
To make travelers think twice.

I walked around assuring wife
That this was just the spot
To have a picnic lunch for two
And keep from getting hot.
When finally my wife agreed,
I grabbed our bag and tea,
Then we both climbed without a scratch
And sat under the tree.

My wife pulled out the sandwiches
While I pulled out a sheet;
Which was bright red but grassy so
I waved it with a beat.
No sooner had I swung the cloth
Than when I heard a sound;
And saw a bull come charging me
Over a hilly mound.

I yelled to wife to get up fast
Then we both jumped the fence;
Escaping in the nick of time -
The moment was intense.
We both saw bull wrapped in the sheet
Who rushed around all mad;
He stunk while trampling sandwiches
And cans of tea we had.

I saw my wife start laughing then,
Which made me chuckle, too;
As I could see the thing I did
Was dumb for me to do.
We got our things and drove on home
With tales for us to tell;
Recounting where most certainly
The bull and sheet did smell.

No Food For Thought

Once there was a girl and boy
Who didn't do their chores;
When Mom and Dad would ask their help,
They'd hide behind locked doors.

Every time their Mom would ask
The clothes be put away,
Each child would hide back in a room
To color or to play.

When their Dad would come to them
To take out all the trash,
The children would not do the chore,
And vanish in a flash.

Repeatedly the parents said
To sweep the Persian rug;
But every time the hint was made,
The kids just gave a shrug.

Soon the Mom and Dad got tired
And made a solemn vow;
That children who would not do chores
Would not get any chow.

An ice cream truck just happened by
With music down the street;
The children ran to Mom and Dad
And asked them for a treat.

The parents laughed and said to them,
"We're sorry. That's too bad!
Since none of you did chores today,
No ice cream will be had."

Then later on at dinner time,
Mom made a great beef stew;
But when the children came to eat,
Mom said, "There's none for you."

The children went to bed that night
Without even a bean;
And said, while crying in their beds,
"Why are our folks so mean?"

Then in the morn, a marvel came
Which made both parents cry;
They saw the clothes all put away
And plates washed clean and dry.

The trash was out, the rugs were swept,
And breakfast on the table;
But with the food, a note was laid
With hearts upon its label.

The note was from both kids that read,
"We love you. We were wrong.
From now on we will do our chores
With gladness and a song."

Then And There

Cast out all burdens of sorrow
Throw down all weights of despair
Place all of yourself in the hands of God;
He will lift you - then and there.

Hold back from speaking in anger
Don't strike when life isn't fair
When you're in conflict ask the Lord for peace;
He will calm you - then and there.

A deed of love is eternal
A word of love is God's style
Keep doing and speaking the things of God;
You'll see changes and His smile.

Spread joy to those who have fallen
Bring hope to those who're in need
Shine bright for the Lord as you live your life;
God will help you plant His seed.

The world around us is sinful
Our towns need Jesus to share
Whatever you do, wherever you go;
He will use you - then and there.

So seek a heart found in Jesus
Let Him remove every snare
No matter what things you've done in your past;
He will heal you - then and there.

Signs Of A Teenager

A bed is not made
Some clothes on the floor
A radio blasts
Inside a bath door
The scent of cologne
Is thick in the air
And several wet towels are
Draped over a chair.

The phone's off the hook
Loose change is about
The washer is full
Old sandals thrown out
Coke cans on a box
With pizza devoured
And stacks of rock music
Both scattered and towered.

The laptop is on
With book bag on bed
Class notes spread around
With things to be read
Some trophies on shelf
Torn pictures on wall
And duffle bag holding
A worn soccer ball.

How time has not changed
The signs of a teen
With few things in place
And nothing pristine
But parents all know
When all's said and done
There's no greater joy to raise
Daughter or son.

Love Of My Life

Your love always makes me shine as my wife
I'm so glad that you are mine in my life
Please come tell me one more time dearest wife
That you'll live and die with me.

You bow and think of me in daily prayer
I watch your face and see an angel there
God knows you hold the key to heaven's stair -
You are Christ's and now you're free.

I love to hear you laugh out loud
And love to see you smile
I wish that I could stop all time
To cherish them awhile.

Though cupboards may be short of food
And savings may be low
I am the richest man on earth
Because you love me so.

I want to see your face in glory's light
I want to share his grace in heaven's sight
God has a final place reserved tonight
If he calls us home to be.

If tomorrow takes me home precious wife
Remember you're not alone in this life
I'll be waiting at God's throne lovely wife
To hold you eternally.

Reading Bedtime Stories

Fairies dusting sleepy lashes
Pirates wearing black eye patches
Gargoyles with an egg that hatches -
Once upon a time.

Giants drinking ale in flagons
Princes fighting mighty dragons
Settlers riding in their wagons -
Once upon a time.

Bedtime stories read together
With our kids in beds of feather
Help them sleep in any weather -
Heads on their pillow.

Stories with a moral ending
Help a child grow up while sending
Points to learn while comprehending -
Being a hero.

So retell Revere's night of riding
Rahab with the spies in hiding
Great men who were law abiding -
Once upon a time.

Battles fought although so gory
Saul's bright light conversion story
Jesus raised from death to glory -
Once upon a time.

Lllamas

Yes, one-L lama,
Is a priest and
Two-L llama,
Is a beast but
Send O. Nash's
Silk pajama,
Since he bet in
His "The Lama,"
That there was
No three-L lllama.
Yes there is - I must inseast!
I confirmed this from my momma,
Who looked up this type of drama;
That there is a three-L lllama -
It's what firemen love the least.
Not intending to alama -
With respect to the deceased.

*This poem written
in loving memory of
Ogden Nash (1902-1971)
and his poem
"The Lama."*

Little Time Is All We Have

Our lives are only specks of time to God
Compared to where we spend eternity;
The paths we choose, while walking on this sod,
Are steered by whom we follow fervently.
How did you spend your precious time today?
What were the things you did that made God glad?
Did you show love for Him in every way,
Or did your lack of love make others sad?
Don't let the fallen angel of all time
Deceive and make you think you have awhile
To serve your God - for this is the great crime
That takes a soul from grace at the last trial.
So turn your heart to Christ today, and run!
Don't stand in fields like cattle in a herd;
Go forth with love! Your mission has begun,
And reach for souls with Jesus through His word!

You Made My Whole Week

All the things you did
That struck me as nice
When you gave your time
Without thinking twice
Working hard to serve
Blowing me away -
You made my whole week
While only Monday.

When you let me pass
In the grocery line
With a cart of food
I thought you were kind
But when no cards worked
You stepped into pay -
And made my whole week
While only Tuesday.

When my car broke down
On a winding road
You called a garage
To have my car towed
Then you drove me home
Though it was a way -
And made my whole week
While only Wednesday.

When my wife was sick
You came to my side
Being there for me
With heart open wide
Bringing food to eat
And a large bouquet -
You made my whole week
While only Thursday.

When I lost my job
You made inquiries
Through some friends of yours
In some companies
Then I got work soon
Since you called each day -
You made my whole week;
Thank God for Friday.

When I moved to town
You helped me unload
A truck full of stuff
And trailer it towed
You worked tirelessly
And I'm glad to say -
You made my whole week
On that Saturday.

I then had to ask
What moved you to be
A servant to all
Who serves selflessly.
You led me to Christ
Whom now I obey -
He changed my whole life
On Easter Sunday.

I Love It When

I love it when I get you sweetheart
All to myself;
To take a walk -
To sit and talk -
About our lives and health.

I love it when I take you sweetheart
Out for a ride;
To drive around -
To get unwound -
With just you by my side.

I know you are so busy
Slaving away;
You wash -
You mend -
You cook -
You tend -
And go to work each day.

I know you are an angel
Sent from above;
You serve -
You care -
You heal -
You share -
God's precious gift of love.

I love it when I have you sweetheart
Close in my arms;
Your kiss, your face,
Your warm embrace,
Are some of your great charms.

I'll love it when in heaven sweetheart
God will make things new;
I'll be in white,
And what a sight
When He puts wings on you.

More Faithful Than

More faithful than the sun each day
Will rise to warm and light the way
To every road that it will reach
And every cloud its rays will breach
That paints each lake and sea with white
Until it fades away from sight;
More faithful than the sun is true -
Is the great love God has for you.

More faithful than the seas subside
That pull back at the morning tide
Which leave on shore its lovely shells
Of conchs and clams for market sales
Along with hermit crabs in sand
That children love to scoop in hand;
More faithful than the tides will strew -
Is the great love God has for you.

More faithful than the stars that shine
And form each constellation sign;
Like those of great and little bears
That chart true north with careful stares,
Which help each captain through the night
Sail straight on course until the light;
More faithful than a star is blue -
Is the great love God has for you.

More faithful than the moon that glows
While giving nightly moonlight shows
That goes from new to full in size
While luminescence fills the skies
It keeps on shining on each lawn
Until the sun comes at the dawn;
More faithful than the moon is new -
Is the great love God has for you.

The poems in this book were set in 10 point
Century Schoolbook.

OTHER POETRY BY PAUL RAY

If you enjoyed

Open Thoughts
PASSAGES OF POETRY

you may also like

Upwords
A FLIGHT OF POETRY
ISBN 978-0-578-03647-2

and

Scattered Glimpses
LEAVES OF POETRY
ISBN 978-0-578-03646-5
available online at lulu.com

www.ingramcontent.com/pod-product-compliance
Lightning Source LLC
Chambersburg PA
CBHW030156070426
42447CB00031B/717